YOU HAVE IT IN YOU! WORKBOOK

EMPOWERED TO DO THE IMPOSSIBLE

SHERYL BRADY

Howard Books
A Division of Simon & Schuster, Inc.
New York   Nashville   London   Toronto   Sydney   New Delhi

Howard Books
A Division of Simon & Schuster, Inc.
1230 Avenue of the Americas
New York, NY 10020

First Howard Books trade paperback edition October 2013

HOWARD and colophon are trademarks of Simon & Schuster, Inc.

For information about special discounts for bulk purchases,
please contact Simon & Schuster Special Sales at 1-866-506-1949
or business@simonandschuster.com.

The Simon & Schuster Speakers Bureau can bring authors to your live event. For
more information or to book an event, contact the Simon & Schuster Speakers
Bureau at 1-866-248-3049 or visit our website at www.simonspeakers.com.

Designed by Davina Mock-Maniscalco

Manufactured in the United States of America

10   9   8   7   6   5   4   3   2   1

Library of Congress Cataloging-in-Publication data is available.

ISBN 978-1-4767-5753-7
ISBN 978-1-4516-7412-5 (ebook)

Also by Sheryl Brady

You Have It In You!

CONTENTS

Your Mission Is NOT Impossible!

Dear Friend,

You never know when God will present you with an extraordinary invitation to discover more of the treasure buried inside you. It may come through the excitement of an unexpected opportunity, a time to step up and work harder than you've ever worked. It might be through the excruciating pain of a devastating trial, a situation you don't understand even as you keep pushing through it. It could be through that mother of invention—necessity—that you find out what you're really made of.

Regardless of the particular crossroads, we're constantly forced to make choices about the path and steps we'll take. Whether it's a job promotion that scares us to death or a battle with a physical illness that takes us to death's door, how will we face such adversity? Will we resign ourselves to going through the motions of a desperate, defeated existence? Or will we allow God to transform our challenges into opportunities for personal expansion?

Often in these life-changing, heart-stopping moments of change, we feel overwhelmed and afraid we don't have what it takes. We fear we don't have the strength, the faith, the courage, the resolve, the patience, or the hope to overcome the huge obstacles in our path. We figure that since we're not superheroes, there's no way we can power through such enormous adversity.

But God doesn't need superheroes—He needs only you.

Of course, superheroes continue to dominate blockbuster movies and many of our favorite television shows. Alone or in teams, male or female, young or old, they suit up in colorful costumes, sometimes made of steel or iron, and find new ways to save the world and thwart the evil schemes of their archrivals. Whether they rely on high-tech gadgets or another planet's science, whether their powers are physical or psychological, these heroes often entertain and sometimes inspire us.

Ultimately, however, they don't have what's required to do the impossible: faith in Christ, trust in God, and reliance on the Holy Spirit. To find these kinds of heroes, we need look no further than the pages of God's Word. There we'll find women overcoming loss, poverty, prostitution, slavery, and infertility. There we'll find men triumphing over foreign armies, famine, false accusations, and floodwaters. And in their stories, what's most amazing is that these men and women have no superpowers. In virtually all cases, they are incredible underdogs, the outcasts and outsiders of their communities, facing overwhelming odds.

Just like you and me.

In You Have It in You!, I explore the lives of these heroes of the faith, some of the Bible's most talented, faithful, and amazing people. Through their stories, we see that they didn't know they had it in them, either— not until God revealed the truth about their identities and abilities to them, often in the midst of perilous trials and challenging situations. How could Ruth believe that she had the resilience to start over after losing everything? How could a humble shepherd boy named David understand that inside him was a slayer of giants? How could a mighty leader's little maid display a humble heart that led to healing?

Like these heroes of our faith, all of us have unclaimed abilities waiting to be discovered. We don't have to be superheroes with high-definition, larger-than-life, three-dimensional IMAX powers. We simply have to be ourselves. God wants to peel away the layers we often try to hide behind, dissolve the excuses we use as camouflage, and reveal the beauty of our true selves.

As a complement to my book, in the pages that follow I want to challenge you to reconsider the way you see yourself and to reframe your understanding of why you are here. Through reflecting honestly, journaling, meditating on Scripture, and engaging in prayer, you will strengthen your awareness of how God made you and how He wants you to serve His kingdom. As you use this workbook, my hope is that you will be inspired to reconsider your current challenges as opportunities for personal growth and a deeper, richer relationship with God.

Do you know what you're made of? More importantly, do you want to discover the many strengths lying dormant inside of you just waiting to be discovered? The talents waiting to be honed and *utilized? The courage that can fuel a confidence you've never experienced? Then this workbook is for you!*

My prayer is that you will finish this workbook with a new perspective on all God has brought you through, a greater awareness of all you've accomplished and endured, and a revelation of confidence that comes from excavating the buried treasure within your soul. You may not know you have it in you, but God does! If you want to experience His power to do what seems impossible, your journey begins now.

Sheryl Brady

INTRODUCTION

The Significance of Feeling Insignificant

Do You Have What It Takes?

Before you begin: Please familiarize yourself with the Introduction to *You Have It in You!*, The Significance of Feeling Insignificant, on pages xi–xxiv.

L IFE RARELY SENDS us a job description of the traits needed to survive and thrive. It might be nice if we knew what we were getting into beforehand, but so far I haven't experienced it. "Wanted: Strong, dynamic woman of God to preach, teach, and pastor around the world." While I'd like to say that I'd be too humble to apply for such a position, the truth is that I'd probably be too scared!

And yet, amazingly enough, what I find myself doing now

is beyond my wildest dreams. If you had told me years ago what I would be doing today, I never would have believed you. And yet, God knew all along that each trial, each challenge, each advancement was just one more step on the path that He had predestined for me.

You see, God knows what's way down deep inside us even when we can't see it, feel it, or even imagine it. He knows because He created us! As our loving Heavenly Father, He wants us to experience the fullness of the life that He made us to live. But the only way to live this way is to trust Him through every step.

As Peter saw Jesus walk on the waves of the water, we must keep our eyes focused on Him and not look down. Because when we start thinking too much and looking at how we're doing something impossible, that's when we rely on our own power and fail. We begin to drown in the deep end of our own disappointment, afraid and uncertain about how to get back on our feet.

To begin your journey of experiencing the power of God that makes all things possible, I encourage you to consider your present location. And in order to know where you are, it's important to know where you've been, where God has taken you. Just as I shared about how meeting Bishop Jakes in Cleveland was a divine appointment with my future destiny, I still had no idea then how it would lead to his invitation for me to pastor at the Potter's House of North Dallas. But looking back, I can see how God used each experience along the way—both the trials and the triumphs, the anguish and the achievements—to prepare me for doing what once seemed impossible.

I'm convinced this is how God works. We can't usually know what He's up to in the moment, so we have to trust Him and just take the next step (often a baby step) of faith. And in order to do that, we have to be honest about what we're feeling and where we see ourselves. So let's get you started by answering the following questions.

The Power of Reflection

How would you describe your present situation in life? Check all of the following that apply:

Complacent ✓

Afraid of the future ....

Facing a trial ....

Blessed but anxious ✓

Angry and upset   ....

Confused   ....

Disappointed   ....

Excited   ....

Enjoying new responsibilities   ✓.............

Spiritually adrift   ....

Resigned to resentment   ....

Starting over   ....

Storm-tossed   ....

Overall, do you feel more overwhelmed by the opportunities you're facing or more burdened by the baggage of painful challenges?

....

....

....

....

....

....

....

....

Describe your opportunities or challenges. Try to think of a metaphor or image that captures the essence of what you're feeling about your present circumstance. Does it feel more like the desert or a spring shower? More like a visit to a foreign country or a trip to visit your childhood home?

....

....

....

....

....

....

As you look back over your life, how has God led you to this current crossroads?

....

....

....

....

....

....

Where have you glimpsed His presence and experienced His blessings and provisions?

....

....

....

....

....

....

....

....

How has God communicated with you in order to lead you to your current situation?

....

....

....

....

....

....

What do you feel you need most from God right now? Clarity? Peace? Guidance? Direction? Something else?

....

....

....

The Power of His Word

Spend some time meditating on this verse: "And we know that all things work together for good to those who love God, to those who are called according to His purpose" (Rom. 8:28 NKJV).

You may want to look at other translations of it and compare them. And you might also consider printing it on a card or sticky note and posting it on your bathroom mirror or in your car or at your desk. Listen for the personal message that God wants to reveal to you through this verse right now.

The Power to Change

If you could change one thing about yourself, what would it be? Why? How would this change make you better suited to serve God?

....

....

....

....

....

....

If you're serious about wanting to discover more about all that God has placed inside you, then committing to complete this workbook can help. How often do you plan to work on the readings and exercises here? Will you be doing this process alone or with a small group?

....

....

....

....

....

....

....

....

How can completing this workbook make you more aware of what God is doing in your life right now? What other hopes do you have for what this process can accomplish?

....

....

....

....

....

....

....

The Power of Prayer

At the end of each chapter, I'll encourage you to spend some time in prayer. To help get you started, I'll provide a sample prayer, but please don't feel locked in to using it. There are no "right words" or magic formulas for talking to God. He simply wants us to open our hearts to Him, to tell Him our thoughts and feelings, and to listen to what He wants to share with us. So use the prayers provided as a guide, but most importantly, simply spend some time talking to your Father— even five minutes can make a huge difference in your day.

Lord, You know how unsteady I feel right now. You know all the events and circumstances that currently challenge me and cause me to stumble. I want to trust You and just take the next step You reveal to me. I may not feel as if I have what it takes to go through this current situation, but I know You do. And I know You do indeed work all things for good. As I look back, I see so many times when You have sustained me, blessed me, and encouraged me. Thank You for loving me, for creating me for a divine purpose that You continue to reveal to me. Please use this workbook and my time with You to further reveal where I'm going and what You would have me do along the way. Amen.

Most of us have no idea what we are truly capable of accomplishing—or perhaps more accurately, what God has created us to achieve, with him as our power source.

—*You Have It in You!*, page xxiii

CHAPTER ONE

THE GRACE TO START OVER

Having the Resilience of Ruth

Before you begin: Please familiarize yourself with Chapter 1 of *You Have It in You!*, pages 1–24.

O UR LIVES ARE constantly in motion. If we're not relocating our home to a different part of the city, another state, or across the country, then we're starting over at a new job, a new church, or in a new relationship. Some people seem to thrive on these cycles of fresh starts and new beginnings. Others like to stay put and enjoy the constancy, the security, and the certainty that come with familiar territory. I can relate to both, and the reality is that we all must learn how to live with both of these often opposing forces in our lives.

On the one hand, we all long for home, a place of love and belonging—the place, a famous poet once said, "where they have to take you in." We also long for something new and exciting, something fresh to stimulate our growth and prevent us from becoming stale and complacent. Most of all, we long to control the decisions that determine when we'll stay and when we'll go. But rarely do we have such a luxury. Most of the time we must consider many other variables: our family's needs, our finances, our relationships, our church community, our career opportunities, our own sense of happiness, and, ultimately, where we sense the Lord is leading.

The Power of Reflection

As I share in Chapter 1, I had so many fears and uncertainties about our move from Raleigh back to Dallas: *What will the future hold for us in this new land? Will the blessings that are so obviously on our lives go with us? Will the goodness of the Lord taste as good to us in Texas as it does in North Carolina? Am I even capable of doing this?* Even though moving can be bittersweet, we have to remember that God already has something much bigger set in motion: our destinies as His sons and daughters.

When was the last time you had to start over? When were you forced to move a major part of your life— your home, your job, your church—from one place to another?

New Church. New Way of Worshipping. New People and responsibilities.

A new-born Child at age 57.

Based on your experience with that move, where are you now: restless and eager for a new adventure? Or weary and desperate to stay put and enjoy your current location?

....

....

....

....

....

What's one area of your life that you wish you could start over? What's preventing you from creating a fresh start?

....

....

....

....

....

....

....

....

Where do you sense God is leading you to make a change? What will you have to give up in order to move forward on the path to which He's calling you?

....

....

....

....

....

....

....

As Ruth embarked on a new frontier of unknowns, she was primarily motivated by her relationships and the love she felt for two people: her deceased husband, Mahlon, and her mother-in-law, Naomi. In fact, as we see in Ruth 1, Ruth clearly had a choice, given freely by Naomi, who likely felt as if she had no other option but to return to Bethlehem after the loss of her husband and both sons. Naomi begged her young daughters-in-law to remain there in Moab, their homeland.

While Orpah decided that this was, in fact, the best path for her, Ruth became only more determined to stay with Naomi and help her face whatever challenges the future revealed.

Have you ever had to take a leap of faith in order to follow someone you loved? If not a physical move, then a move of your heart? In other words, have you ever had to choose between playing it safe and walking in uncharted territory?

....

....

....

....

....

....

....

....

....

....

Who has offered to walk with you down some of the then-unknown roads of your past? Did you accept their offer or drive them away by being cold and aloof?

....

....

....

....

....

....

If you accepted their offer, was it difficult to do? What got in the way and nearly prevented you from accepting their offer to be with you?

....

....

....

....

....

....

....

....

How has your decision to start over in a major area
of your life affected those around you—family,
close friends, coworkers? How have your relationships changed due to starting over?

....

....

....

....

....

....

....

....

Each of us has a choice every day either to remain in the Moab of our lives, the place with people just like us, the place where we've always belonged, the place that makes no real demands on us, or to embark on a journey of faith into a new country.

—*You Have It in You!*, page 15

The Power of His Word

One of the most amazing truths gleaned from Ruth's story is the way God provides for us when He challenges us to make a move. His provision doesn't mean the move will be easy—often far from it—but it does mean that He never forsakes us. Ruth found herself impoverished in a strange new land, trying to support herself as well as Naomi, who seemed to be losing her battle with bitterness. Ruth never gave up. If she had to glean from the fields after all the others, then she would be grateful for the leftover of the leftovers and make do.

I'm convinced this is what attracted Boaz's attention to this unfamiliar woman who traipsed along behind his workers in the fields: Ruth's resilience. He clearly respected her efforts enough to tell his workers to leave plenty for her to pick up. He also treated her with kindness and told her how to remain safe. Even before the full extent of their entwined destinies became apparent, God was providing for the needs of Ruth and Naomi. It wasn't a fairy tale where Ruth just had to wait for the prince to show up. It was a daily date with destiny, simply doing what she knew how to do.

If you didn't read the story of Ruth when you read Chapter 1, then read it now. If you did read the story of Ruth before, reread it now in your favorite version of Scripture. What part of her story moves you the most? Why? What is it about that part of her journey that resonates so powerfully with your own?

....

....

....

....

....

....

What frightens you the most about moving forward to the place God is presently calling you to discover? What must you release in order to embrace what He wants to give you?

....

....

....

....

....

....

....

....

....

....

....

....

....

So Boaz took Ruth and she became his wife; and
when he went in to her, the Lord gave her conception,
and she bore a son.

Then the women said to Naomi, "Blessed be the
Lord, who has not left you this day without a close
relative; and may his name be famous in Israel!

"And may he be to you a restorer of life and a
nourisher of your old age; for your daughter-in-law,
who loves you, who is better to you than seven sons, has
borne him."

(Ruth 4:13–15 NKJV)

The Power to Change

Naomi and her family had to leave their homeland in Bethlehem initially in order to survive physically. After losing her husband and sons, Naomi then had to return home in order to survive physically and emotionally. To enter the next season of our lives, we often have to leave behind our current surroundings, if not literally then often symbolically. Similarly, if we're serious about discovering all that God has placed within us, we often must let go of things that are getting in the way.

What do you need to release in your life and move away from in order to grow closer to God today? What's He calling you to leave behind so you can move forward?

....

....

....

....

....

....

What are you most afraid of losing as you follow God into this next season of your life? How can your fears draw you closer to Him? What step do you need to take today in order to trust Him more?

....

....

....

....

....

....

....

....

The Power of Prayer

Before you spend some time in prayer, I encourage
you to think about the ways God has provided for
you in the past when you've started new ventures.
How has he guided you to where you are presently?
What has He provided to get you here? Where do
you sense Him leading you as you anticipate the
future?

....

....

....

....

....

....

....

....

God, I know you are my Father and You always have my best interests at heart. I know I can trust You to guide me toward my destiny. Just as Ruth had to remain patient, hardworking, and faithful before she discovered the joys of your blessings, I pray that I may also remain diligent and trust where you are leading me. You know my needs better than I do, but from where I stand, I really need _____. Please continue to provide for me, Lord, and to show me where to look for the spilled barley on the ground in my own life. Help me to find the relationships you would have me invest in the most. I thank You, God, that no matter how scary it might feel right now, You know what You've placed inside me. Help me to know what You already know. Help me to be resilient. Amen.

> *There are things that you and I must do to provoke the release of God's purpose in our lives. We may not know all of what God has placed within us, but we must be open to find it and, against all odds, continue to move forward.*
>
> —*You Have It in You!*, page 23

CHAPTER TWO

TREASURE IN A TRAMP'S HOUSE

Taking Risks Like Rahab

Before you begin: Please familiarize yourself with Chapter 2 of *You Have It in You!*, pages 25–41.

O NE OF THE best, yet hardest, life lessons I've learned is to view adversity as opportunity. When something doesn't go the way I wanted or expected, I've learned to redefine my expectations. It's not always easy, but over the years, as I've watched God turn my mistakes into His masterpieces, I've realized that just because circumstances challenge me, I don't have to back away. Just the opposite, in fact! Problems, conflicts, and mistakes require us to draw on what God has given us as well as to depend on Him for what He's about to give us.

When life is going a million miles a minute, though, it can be so tempting to throw up our hands in despair. We might lose our jobs, get passed over for the promotion, see our children struggle with addictions, argue with our spouses, and wonder how all the bills are going to be paid. In the midst of such a riptide of responsibility, it's hard to stay afloat. But this is when God Himself becomes our anchor. This is when He asks us to let go of our own attempts at making things work and allow Him to reveal His plan—including our part in it. Sometimes our hardest moments are the ones that help us to discover what's really inside us.

The Power of Reflection

We may not know we have what it takes to survive the challenges we currently face, but God does. We may think it's too late for us or that we're not good enough. We may feel as though God could never use someone who's messed up as much as we have. But the story of Rahab reminds us that it's never too late: there's always treasure inside us waiting to come out. No matter how tarnished we may feel on the outside, God has placed His greatest investment inside us. We'll need to take some risks along the way, but the discoveries we'll make—about ourselves, about what we're made of, about God—are priceless.

What challenges are you facing? What obstacles are blocking the route you had planned on taking to achieve your next major goal?

....

....

....

....

....

....

....

....

....

....

....

....

What's your usual response to such roadblocks in life? Anger? Frustration? Fear? Confusion? Disappointment? Describe how you usually handle a day when things don't go your way.

....

....

....

....

....

....

....

....

As you reflect on challenges you've overcome, consider how they have helped you grow. What did God teach you about yourself, and about Him, through those adversities?

....

....

....

....

....

....

....

....

Choose one of the current challenges you face and describe how it's blocking your path. What are the opportunities that it's also providing? How are you being invited to grow in a new direction?

....

....

....

....

....

....

....

....

....

Rahab was clearly a shrewd businesswoman who knew how to handle the politics, both personal and professional, of living in Jericho. Still, when the spies came knocking on her door, she had to act fast and trust her gut. There was no time to analyze facts, research best options, and make scientific conclusions. As I share in Chapter 2, I'm convinced that God had been working on softening Rahab's heart prior to that fateful knock on her door.

He had already planted seeds of His love for her so that when the time came, her instincts would be to step out in faith, to take a chance on His followers and their obedience to Him. Somehow, the two seem to go hand in hand: we trust God and take a risk to obey Him, which deepens our trust, which then allows Him to ask us to take a greater risk.

Why do you think a woman in Rahab's position would be willing to harbor spies and deceive her city's officials? Do you think her decision was more practical—to save her own skin and her family's— or more fueled by faith (trusting in this new God she was discovering)?

....

....

....

....

....

....

....

....

When have you experienced a situation that required you to trust God more than the reality sur-
rounding you? How did you determine when and
where to take this risk?

....

....

....

....

....

....

....

....

Rahab easily could have allowed her role and reputation as a harlot to prevent her from acting on her newfound faith. When have your role and reputation complicated the risk you felt God calling you to take?

....

....

....

....

....

....

....

....

How have the betrayals of others in the past affected your willingness to take a risk? Why does it feel harder to risk now than when you were younger?

....

....

....

....

....

....

....

....

Whatever Rahab had been through, it was really not that different from what many of us have been through. . . . The good news is that Rahab's story allows us to see that for every disappointment, God has a divine appointment!

—*You Have It in You!*, page 34

The Power of His Word

Rahab's remarkable story teaches us never to discount how much God loves an underdog. She reminds us, as do so many saints of the faith, that it's what's inside us that counts.

And drawing on what's inside us, we're able to take risks that may frighten, amaze, confuse, and even terrify us when we stop to think about them. If we stay in our heads and try to figure out the next step of faith we're called to take, we'll likely become paralyzed. So often these risks are irrational, illogical, and unbelievable—yes, sometimes they even seem a little crazy!

Did Rahab really believe that throwing a red cord out her window would save her family amid the utter devastation occurring around her as the Hebrew army invaded Jericho? And better yet, would these foreigners really honor their promise to her and recognize the red cord as a sign of favor and protection? As the men and women of her homeland screamed around her, as fire swept through the city walls, as destruction loomed on every side—yes, she believed. She did what she had been asked to do. And she and her family were saved.

Each of us has our own scarlet cord that we must hang from our window. Each of us has something God is asking us to entrust to Him, something that requires a step of faith on our part, a risk that stretches us beyond our comfort zone. We all need God to rescue us and redeem us on a daily basis. But sometimes in order for us to discover His mercy, we must first get out of our heads and into our hearts.

Did you read the story of Rahab (Joshua 2–6) when you read Chapter 2? If not, then read through it carefully in your favorite version of the Bible. What surprises you most about her story? What troubles you the most about it?

....

....

....

....

....

....

In what ways can you identify with Rahab and the dilemma she faced? Where is God presently asking you to step out in faith even though it may seem a little crazy? How are the risks you're being asked to take similar to Rahab's?

....

....

....

....

....

....

....

....

"Now therefore, I beg you, swear to me by the Lord, since I have shown you kindness, that you also will show kindness to my father's house, and give me a true token, and spare my father, my mother, my brothers, my sisters, and all that they have, and deliver our lives from death."

So the men answered her, "Our lives for yours, if none of you tell this business of ours. And it shall be, when the Lord has given us the land, that we will deal kindly and truly with you."

(Josh. 2:12–14 NKJV)

The Power to Change

Rahab may have wondered why God chose her, out of all the citizens of Jericho, to use for His purposes and to save from destruction. Most of us may struggle with this same question from time to time—and we'll never know completely. Take a few moments and write a brief description of how you think God sees you right now, right here, today.

....

....

....

....

....

....

....

....

....

....

How is this view you've just written supported by God's Word? In other words, if you're totally honest with yourself, how much of this view is your own estimation of yourself rather than God's?

....

....

....

....

....

....

....

....

If you believe that God loves you and has placed treasure inside you, what action do you need to take today to uncover those riches? What's one small risk you can take to demonstrate your trust in Him?

....

....

....

....

....

....

....

The Power of Prayer

Lord, You know that my life has been far from perfect and that there have been so many times when I've wanted to give up. But I know that Your purposes are so much bigger than what I can see. Help me to trust You with all areas of my life, even when it's painful and I can't understand all that's going on around me. And, God, please show me what risk you want me to take, what scarlet cord you want me to hang from my window, in order to please You, to glorify You, and to discover more of the treasure You've placed inside me. Thank You for loving me so much and for always rescuing me in my time of trouble. Amen.

Even if you don't know your own self-worth, you have treasure inside you that is beginning to sparkle in the sun.

—*You Have It in You!*, page 41

CHAPTER THREE

I'M NOT DRUNK— I'M DESPERATE!

Persisting with the Passion of Hannah

Before you begin: Please familiarize yourself with Chapter 3 of *You Have It in You!*, pages 43–60.

W<small>E ALL HAVE</small> dreams inside us. Some of them have been growing in us since childhood and continue to call us forward in pursuit of their fulfillment. They might be dreams of completing a degree, starting a business, or creating a family.

Other dreams seem to have come and gone, tainted by failed attempts and missed opportunities. Perhaps one day we realized that our talent alone wasn't enough to catapult us into professional sports or the musical career we coveted.

But that doesn't mean we must abandon our love of football or the joy we get from music. These dreams still burn inside us but have been reduced from the passionate goal that once blazed to nothing more than faint embers. But we have to keep the fire alive. The Bible tells us that "hope deferred makes the heart sick" (Prov. 13:12 NIV), reminding us that we must never give up on the longings of our hearts.

When we really want something, it's helpful to consider our motives. Do we truly feel compelled to write, to speak, to teach, to paint, to sew, or whatever it is because that's our purpose? Or because we just want to have our fifteen minutes in the spotlight and make money? There's nothing wrong with success, but if that's the only desire girding the foundation of our dreams, then it may not be strong enough to support us.

The Power of Reflection

As we grow older and more mature in our faith (we hope!), then our dreams may change, but they're still inside us. From my experience, when we follow the Lord's leading, our dreams are refined and redefined. They become aligned with the direction of our divine destinies. As we discover what God has placed inside us, we realize that we're most content when our dreams mesh with His purposes. He's not going to ask us to do something we were not created or equipped to do. The more we allow God to stretch us, the more we understand that He is the One who has planted our true longings deep inside us.

Scripture tells us, "For where your treasure is, there your heart will be also" (Matt. 6:21 NIV). What treasure is your heart pursuing today? What is the first and foremost desire of your heart right now?

....

....

....

....

....

....

....

....

....

As you think over your life, what's the most important thing you've ever asked God to give you? Did He give it to you the way you expected? Looking back from where you are now, how do you feel about your request?

....

....

....

....

....

....

....

What have you been asking God for most frequently over the past few weeks? Why do you desire this particular request? How would your life be different if He gave it to you today?

....

....

....

....

....

....

....

....

Describe your most fervent lifelong dream. Don't
worry if it feels silly or over the top. If you've always
wanted to host your own talk show, put it down. If
there's a special place you've dreamed about visit-
ing your whole life, jot down the details that cause
this place to appeal to you. If you want to change
careers, list the qualities of the new field that draw
you to it.

....

....

....

....

....

....

....

....

Hannah's passionate persistence remains incredibly relevant for us today as we discover new things inside ourselves. Her story gives us several clues about what it means to long for something with our whole hearts and how to handle the period of waiting before we receive it. I'm struck by her humility, her willingness to be so desperate in her pleas for a baby that she didn't care what others thought. After all, she was so passionate in her prayers to God that the priest mistakenly thought she was drunk!

She knew that the starting point is simply recognizing what we want and giving voice to this desire before the Lord. Hannah didn't know if her request would come to pass or not; she knew simply that she had nowhere else to go, no one else to turn to who could fulfill her heart's desire. So often we work hard and then harder to achieve our goals. We manipulate situations to our advantage to get ahead and try to control all the variables involved. While we must certainly work and do our part, ultimately it's up to God. If we're not turning to Him to meet us in the longings of our hearts, then we will never be satisfied, no matter how many of our dreams come to pass.

Have you ever wanted something so badly you were willing to humble yourself the way Hannah did? Have you ever truly begged God to give you something your heart longed to have? Regardless of how He answered your prayer, what did you learn from that experience?

....

....

....

....

....

....

....

....

....

....

How do you usually discern whether a desire is your own selfish goal or is of God? Before you ask God for something, how do you go about examining your motives? Is there someone you talk with, a period of prayer you like to reflect upon, a favorite passage of Scripture you like to recall?

....

....

....

....

....

....

....

....

....

....

....

....

What one thing would you currently ask God to remove from your life? It might be a painful physical
disease or injury, a personal addiction, a relational
conflict, or a cloud of depression. If He agreed to
remove it today, what would it be?

....

....

....

....

....

....

....

---

*Most of us have no idea what we are truly capable
of accomplishing—or perhaps more accurately, what
God has created us to achieve, with him as our power
source.*

—*You Have It in You!*, page xxiii

What one thing do you long for God to add to your life? It could be a new job, a special relationship, an increase in joy, peace, finances, or reliable transportation. If you opened your eyes after praying for this addition, what would you see?

....

....

....

....

....

....

....

Too often, we get lost in all the busyness of coming and going and working and starting all over again; sometimes we may not even be sure of what we want. . . . We have to get alone with ourselves and with God to know what we really want.

—You Have It in You!, pages 51–52

The Power of His Word

While Hannah's story has a happy ending, it's important to remember that she suffered for a long time without knowing if she would ever receive what she so wanted. Long before Samuel was conceived, Hannah longed to have a baby with her husband and had to endure the shame and contempt heaped on her by Elkanah's other wife. And she didn't just ask God once or twice and then suddenly become a new mother. This longing was purified with gallons of tears, hundreds—perhaps thousands—of frantic prayers, and untold sleepless nights.

Hannah understood that every dream has a price. She knew deep in her bones that her longing to have a baby of her own was core to her identity, to her very purpose and existence. It wasn't a fleeting moment of "maternal envy" when she saw Elkanah's other wife with a new baby. It was something so strong that she couldn't have let go of it even if she had wanted to. And she embraced this desire by expressing it as persistently and as passionately as she possibly could. She didn't pretend that everything would be okay if she didn't have a baby. She accepted that nothing would be okay!

Sometimes we try to pretend that we don't really want what our hearts know we do. We try to get logical or analytical and talk ourselves out of pursuing our dreams. We allow shame or embarrassment or the perceptions of others to eclipse our longings and throw shadows across our paths.

Read over Hannah's story in 1 Samuel 1. What do you find most encouraging about her story? Why? What disturbs you about her story?

....

....

....

....

....

....

....

What price are you willing to pay in order to re ceive what you long for the most? What do you feel you have already sacrificed in order to pursue the dream God has placed in your heart?

....

....

....

....

....

....

....

....

It must have been tempting for Hannah to want to hold on to her baby son once he finally arrived. Still, she honored her promise to God to dedicate Samuel to serving His kingdom. What has God given you that He's now asking you to give up or pass on to others?

....

....

....

....

....

....

What's the "Hannah-sized" dream that continues to haunt you and requires you to be patient with the Lord's timing?

....

....

....

....

....

....

....

....

....

....

....

....

....

....

And it happened, as she continued praying before the Lord, that Eli watched her mouth. Now Hannah spoke in her heart; only her lips moved, but her voice was not heard. Therefore Eli thought she was drunk. So Eli said to her, "How long will you be drunk? Put your wine away from you!"

But Hannah answered and said, "No, my lord, I am a woman of sorrowful spirit. I have drunk neither wine nor intoxicating drink, but have poured out my soul before the Lord.

"Do not consider your maidservant a wicked woman, for out of the abundance of my complaint and grief I have spoken until now."

Then Eli answered and said, "Go in peace, and the God of Israel grant your petition which you have asked of Him."

And she said, "Let your maidservant find favor in your sight." So the woman went her way and ate, and her face was no longer sad.

(1 Sam. 1:12–18 NKJV)

The Power to Change

Write down in one or two sentences the dream you're still waiting for God to fulfill. Now ask yourself, is this dream just for my own satisfaction? Or is it something that will advance His kingdom and bless others as well?

....

....

....

....

....

....

....

....

On a scale of 1 to 10 (with 1 being not asking God for anything and 10 being asking Him with Hannah's intensity), how dedicated have you been to the process of asking God to fulfill your heart's desire? How often do you pray about it? Have you fasted? Journaled? Discussed with family and loved ones?

....

....

....

....

....

....

....

What one action do you need to take today in order to keep your dream alive?

....

....

....

....

....

....

....

....

The Power of Prayer

Heavenly Father, it's difficult for me to talk about
this desire that remains in my heart. You know how
often I've asked You before to grant this dream.
If You've already answered me and I've missed it,
please tell me again and I'll move on. But if it's
something that I need to keep waiting on, then
please grant me the patience to trust You and Your
timing. I know You've placed this dream inside me
for a reason, and even though I may not think I
have what it takes for my dream to come alive, You
continue to surprise me. Help me not to lose hope
but to persist with the passion of Hannah. Test my
motives, Lord, and allow me to be a good steward
of the many gifts that You bestow upon me. Thank
You for all You've already given me as well as that
which is yet to come. Amen.

> Every dream has a price of some kind, and often our patience is tested and our hearts purified by having to wait.
>
> —*You Have It in You!*, page 54

CHAPTER FOUR

WHO DO YOU THINK YOU ARE?

Wrestling with the Determination of Jacob

Before you begin: Please familiarize yourself with Chapter 4 of *You Have It in You!*, pages 61–82.

I LOVE WATCHING MY grandchildren play dress-up. Trying on different grown-up clothes, making a superhero cape out of a beach towel, or turning an old T-shirt into a party dress, they can pretend to be a variety of people, roles, and characters. While we probably don't have as much fun, most of us continue to wear numerous hats and juggle various, often competing, roles as adults. We're someone's employee and someone else's boss. We're people's spouses and mothers or fathers to our children. We're brothers or sisters to our siblings, sons or daughters to our parents, and best friends to a select handful of others.

We also fit certain demographic labels, as most advertisers are quick to notice. We're female or male, black or white or brown or some amazing combination of skin tones. We're blond or brunette, green- or brown- or blue-eyed. We're in a certain age bracket, a certain professional field or career, and we have attained a particular level of education. Our income, neighborhood, and financial stability also often define us. Even the clothes we wear and the cars we drive contribute something to the identity that forms at the center of all these roles and labels.

But at the end of the day, when those layers have been peeled away, who are we really?

The Power of Reflection

Most people know a lot about themselves, their likes and dislikes, their memorable experiences and painful secrets. And yet many still don't know who they are beyond their Facebook status picture and their occupations. Maybe they're afraid or uncertain of what they'll find beneath the designer clothes and status labels of the props around them. Maybe they feel like posers or frauds, fakes or wannabes. Everyone experiences these feelings at times, but as we gain wisdom and maturity, we learn to appreciate the unique masterpieces that our Creator has made us to be.

When you're forced to introduce yourself in a new situation, what do you usually say? How do you typically present yourself to other people? How self-conscious are you about wanting to create a certain impression or image?

....

....

....

....

....

....

....

....

....

....

How would the people who see you every day—
your family, coworkers, and friends—describe you?
How accurately do you think they see you?

....

....

....

....

....

....

....

List three things your friends and family would be
surprised to know about you. Do they know how
much you love cooking Italian food or watching
tearjerkers on television? Do they know about the
time you traveled across the country?

....

....

....

....

....

....

....

....

....

What aspects of your personality and true identity
do you sometimes try to hide or keep in the back-
ground of others' impressions about you? Why?

....

....

....

....

....

....

....

....

Which of your qualities and traits remain present regardless of the role you're playing? Do you feel as if you have a good idea of who you really are, or do you feel more as if you're still searching to discover your true identity?

....

....

....

....

....

....

....

....

Jacob is one of my favorite people in the Bible because he was always trying to make things happen. Even when God foretold events to him (such as receiving his father's blessing), good old Jake took matters into his own hands to fit his own schedule. Pretty soon, his botched efforts created a pattern of broken relationships and ongoing deception. He probably started to doubt himself and wonder if it was even possible to get back on the right track.

But God didn't leave him to stumble along feeling ashamed of past mistakes. God met Jacob where he was—more specifically, in a wrestling match in the middle of nowhere.

When have you rushed into a situation to try to make things happen your way instead of waiting on God's timing? What was the result?

....

....

....

....

....

....

....

....

Sometimes instead of taking matters into our own hands like Jacob, we wait passively on God to drop blessings into our laps. Are you more prone to try to make things happen or to wait for them to happen to you? How can you use your past experiences to rely on God's timing now?

....

....

....

....

....

....

....

In Chapter 4, I discuss the huge roles that names played in biblical times. Jacob's name meant "heel-chaser" or "trickster," while Israel, his new name, meant one who had "struggled with God and with man and [had] overcome" (Gen. 32:28 NIV). With this in mind, what would your old name be? And based on who God says you are, what is your new name?

....

....

....

....

....

....

....

What weakness in your personality or character often leads you to be less than God wants you to be? What area of your life have you seen God use the most to bless other people, despite any mistakes you may have made?

....

....

....

....

....

....

....

....

Just because you've made a mistake doesn't mean you can't fulfill your God-given destiny. When we ask God to forgive us and show us how to get back on the right path, he's faithful to show us his loving mercy and guide us toward our purpose.

—*You Have It in You!*, page 65

The Power of His Word

If you're like me, you probably don't get on the wrestling mat and square off against someone else that often. In fact, if you're like me, you may not even watch wrestling on TV! Regardless of what our experience may be with the literal activity, we all know what it means to wrestle—

with ourselves, with our loved ones, and with God. Perhaps there's simply no other action word that captures the sheer intensity, the enormous struggle, the emotional grappling, and the ongoing exchange of blows better than *wrestling.*

Jacob understood this concept literally and figuratively. For many years, he had clearly wrestled with his own conscience and with the failures haunting him from his past. And then came the World Wrestling Federation match of his lifetime! Alone in the desert, preparing mentally and emotionally for the meeting before him with his estranged brother, Esau, Jacob found himself drenched in sweat and struggling with a mysterious stranger who clearly knew everything about him. As the two grappled and held, spun and released, then grabbed hold again, Jacob realized this was much more than a friendly grudge match. It was the fight of his life.

If you haven't read the story of Jacob in a while, check out Genesis 27–37. While his life has a certain epic quality to it, Jacob's story remains incredibly personal and relevant to us today. As you consider his life in its entirety, what strikes you about our friend Jacob? What was inside him that he didn't realize until the wrestling match with God occurred?

....

....

....

....

....

....

....

Have you had a once-in-a-lifetime experience like Jacob in which your identity was forever clarified and changed? How does that event continue to impact you today? If there's not been one big event, then what moments in your past have shaped how you see yourself?

....

....

....

....

....

....

....

....

> *Then Jacob was left alone; and a Man wrestled with him until the breaking of day. Now when He saw that He did not prevail against him, He touched the socket of his hip; and the socket of Jacob's hip was out of joint as He wrestled with him.*
>
> *And He said, "Let Me go, for the day breaks."*
>
> *But he said, "I will not let You go unless You bless me!"*
>
> *So He said to him, "What is your name?"*
>
> *He said, "Jacob."*
>
> *And He said, "Your name shall no longer be called Jacob, but Israel; for you have struggled with God and with men, and have prevailed."*
>
> (Gen. 32:24–28 NKJV)

The Power to Change

Sometimes when we feel stuck in life, we're really wrestling with God. We may not understand why we're facing certain circumstances or why God isn't coming through for us the way we were hoping. Many times when we're struggling, I'm convinced it happens to reveal something that we couldn't grasp any other way. As God's children, we can be incredibly stubborn about trying to do things our way and refusing to let go of our selfish, sometimes manipulative ways. Just as Jacob discovered, at times the only way for God to use us as leaders is to reveal our limp.

What's an area of present struggle in your life in which you may be wrestling with God? What might He be trying to teach you through this painful process? What do you continue to cling to rather than give up the fight?

....

....

....

....

....

....

....

....

....

Sometimes after God has revealed more of who we really are, it's difficult to accept our new identity. If you are really the person God says you are, how should this change the way you see yourself? What's one thing you absolutely must do today in order to begin leading with your limp?

....

....

....

....

....

....

....

....

The Power of Prayer

Lord, You know how much I struggle right now. I try not to show it, but You and I both know that it's really hard for me to let go of my past and embrace this new identity You've been revealing to me. Please help me to yield to Your power, to surrender to Your loving embrace, and to receive all You want to give me. I may have trouble seeing myself as Your child, Your servant, Your leader, but please do not let me give up the fight before I find Your favor. Please do not let me walk away without a limp. Strengthen me so that I can fight the good fight and face the future with my new name, my true name, the name that reflects all You have placed inside me. Thank You, Lord, for never leaving me alone in the desert with my past mistakes but instead calling me to be all that You made me to be. Amen.

If you want to fulfill your destiny, if you want to discover your true identity and be called by your God-given name, then you must be willing to wrestle.

—*You Have It in You!*, page 77

CHAPTER FIVE

CALLING COURAGE
OUT OF A COWARD

Fighting with the Courage of Gideon

Before you begin: Please familiarize yourself with Chapter 5 of *You Have It in You!*, pages 83–105.

S O MANY PEOPLE end up in careers or relationships or lives simply by default. When their childhood dreams didn't come true, when Plan A failed them, they didn't know what to do—there was no Plan B. In fact, this may be true of most of us. But when there's no follow-up plan, when disappointment defines us more than our divine destinies do, we can end up settling for whatever comes our way . . . whatever job we can get easily . . . whatever spouse will have us . . . whatever life seems to give us. And then we wonder why God isn't doing more in our lives!

This really bothers me, because based on my experience and what I see in Scripture, God definitely is doing something in all our lives if we can only learn to pay attention and listen. Often God speaks to us, directs us, and reveals what we have inside us, and then we balk and look over our shoulder as if He couldn't possibly be talking to us. We pray for more vibrant, fulfilling, faith-filled lives, and then we remain oblivious to opportunity when that train leaves the station! If we want to discover the extent of all God has placed in us and to tap into Him as our true power source, then we must learn to take God at His word rather than test Him and ask Him to repeat Himself.

The Power of Reflection

In Chapter 5, I share about the spiritual shift that seems to have occurred from my generation to that of my children and grandchildren. When I was growing up, we focused foremost on our salvation and the relationship that we are able to have with God as our Father because of the sacrifice of His Son, Jesus, on the cross. But after this primary relationship was established, we didn't always realize how much God had placed inside us to use for His purposes. When I was a young believer, most of my prayers revolved around my telling God what I wanted instead of listening for what God wanted to tell me. It took a while for me to realize that He had so much more to say to me.

When was the last time you spent at least twenty minutes alone in silence listening for God? Why do you think we often need to stop and pay attention in order to hear and sense what God wants to tell us?

For ~~dinner partners.~~

What message did you receive when you last sensed God speaking to you? What surprised you about this message?

....

....

....

....

....

....

Perhaps you already have a clear message from God about what He wants from you moving forward. While it's wonderful to have a sense of direction and purpose in our lives, God never leaves us to find our own way. What is He asking you to do—perhaps something very small—for Him right now, today?

....

....

....

....

....

....

....

....

When have others spoken into your life, whether
they realized it or not, with messages from God?
When has He used you to speak His truth into
someone else's life? In either case, what was the
impact?

....

....

....

....

....

....

....

The story of Gideon is one of my favorites because of the way it shows an everyday underdog being transformed into a bold warrior for the Lord. Earlier in this workbook, I mentioned the way our culture loves heroes and superheroes who seem larger than life with their displays of amazing strength and powerful gifts. While these heroes can often inspire us, sometimes we focus more on what we perceive as the gap between ourselves and their heroic qualities.

We settle into our routine lives and assume that God could never use us in such a dramatic, life-changing, kingdom-building way. But Gideon reminds us otherwise. Hiding in a hut used for pressing grapes into wine, Gideon had retreated to thresh wheat into flour when God showed up in an unmistakable way. Gideon wasn't expecting to encounter God, but God had a divine appointment with this man whom He addressed as "a mighty warrior."

On a daily basis, how often are you aware of God's presence even amid the details of your life—at work in your office, at home as you do chores, at school as you study, at church as you serve?

....

....

....

....

....

....

....

....

When was the last time God showed up unexpect-
edly—and unmistakably—in an ordinary day? How
did you respond to this divine appointment?

....

....

....

....

....

....

....

....

....

What message did God communicate to you through this latest encounter? How did you feel based on what He expected from you? Was it apparent that He sees more in you than you see in yourself?

....

....

....

....

....

....

....

Like Gideon, we are also God's "mighty warriors." What battle might you presently be called to fight in your life? What needs to change in order for you to fight this battle with the power of the Lord?

....

....

....

....

....

....

....

....

> *None of us has time to waste, and yet so many do it every day by shooting in the dark at destiny, failing to discern the difference between what we want for us and what God has purposed for us.*
>
> —*You Have It in You!*, page 87

The Power of His Word

Gideon's story is not only a testament to the way God uses ordinary people for extraordinary purposes, but it's also a cautionary reminder of the way we often drag our feet and try to test God rather than accept the gifts He offers us. Rather than immediately embrace the reality of his new identity as a leader and warrior, Gideon hemmed and hawed and set out a fleece—not just once but twice—to make sure God really knew what He was doing. No matter how much Gideon may have been willing to trust that God was finally doing something to defend and restore the nation of Israel, he still couldn't accept that God wanted to use him, the youngest member of the weakest tribe, to do it.

Perhaps Gideon had simply accepted the labels that others had assigned to him. After all, he wasn't even out with the other men trying to defend the borders against the Midianites; he was hiding at home doing what was traditionally a task for the women. It seems likely that up until his fateful encounter with God, Gideon didn't think very highly of himself and didn't challenge the way others perceived him. He just went with the flow and allowed others to define him as a passive weakling, someone from whom no one expected much at all.

Read Gideon's story in Judges 6–8 in your favorite version of Scripture. How does Gideon's story compare with what you know of most traditional underdog stories? How does his story compare to where you are in your own life?

....

....

....

....

....

....

....

How are you testing God presently in your own life? Are there areas where you're waiting when you know you should be moving forward obediently?

....

....

....

....

....

....

....

....

What do you think you lack that is necessary to do what God is asking in the current season of your life? In other words, how does God see you (just as He saw Gideon as a mighty warrior and not a wimp) as compared to how you see yourself?

....

....

....

....

....

....

....

Gideon had to face his fears and be willing to put his faith into action. What risks must you take in order to move to the next level where God wants to lead you?

....

....

....

....

....

....

....

....

....

....

....

....

....

....

....

....

And the Angel of the Lord appeared to him, and said to him, "The Lord is with you, you mighty man of valor!"

Gideon said to Him, "O my lord, if the Lord is with us, why then has all this happened to us? And where are all His miracles which our fathers told us about, saying, 'Did not the Lord bring us up from Egypt?' But now the Lord has forsaken us and delivered us into the hands of the Midianites."

Then the Lord turned to him and said, "Go in this might of yours, and you shall save Israel from the hand of the Midianites. Have I not sent you?"

(Judges 6:12–14 NKJV)

The Power to Change

No matter how bruised, disappointed, and discouraged you may be by life's blows, God says you still have what it takes to be His mighty warrior. You may feel weak or weary, timid or tired, but He has equipped you to fight life's battles without giving up. And when He places you in the midst of conflict, you don't have to be afraid or spend time testing Him. You can simply dig deep and exercise your faith by obeying His call and taking action. You may not sense it, but you have the courage and the strength and the power to defeat all adversaries in your path.

What must change in order for you to unleash the warrior God has placed inside you? What step can you take today to embrace the power He's given you?

....

....

....

....

....

What battle are you most afraid of losing in your life? What action would you take today if you trusted God to enable you to conquer all you're facing?

....

....

The Power of Prayer

It's so easy, Lord, to overlook the ways You speak to me and the messages You send. So often I don't expect much to change in my day-to-day life. I get resigned to the way things are and forget that You are always working behind the scenes, both for Your glory and for my good. Please help me to pay attention and listen carefully when I hear Your voice whispering my true identity. Allow me to accept and embrace who You say I am rather than who I feel I've become. And please forgive me when I test You and lay out fleeces to make sure You're really saying what I thought I heard. Give me tenacity to rely on You and Your power alone as the source of all my might. Give me the courage of Gideon so that I can win the battles that I'm facing, knowing that I can more than conquer anything in my path as long as You are with me. Amen.

When God calls us to use what he's placed inside us, we must expect that we will discover new qualities inside ourselves, especially the courage to be our true selves. People may be surprised because of what they've come to expect from us. Yet when we're empowered and unleashed, they're often forced to see us in a new light.

—*You Have It in You!*, page 101

CHAPTER SIX

FINDING FAITH
TO FLOAT

Obeying with the Certainty of Noah

Before you begin: Please familiarize yourself with Chapter 6 of *You Have It in You!*, pages 107–124.

A T SOME POINT in our lives, most of us are required to build something that requires more than our available resources. It may be a start-up business, a new church, a community group, a blended family, or some other endeavor that we must construct from scratch. Many of these "building projects" will demand not only our time, money, and energy, but an investment of our faith as well. These new projects we're called on to construct may not seem to make much sense from other people's viewpoints.

They may tell us there's not enough time, money, space, or volunteers, not enough interest or commitment to build what we're asked to build. We may end up doubting ourselves and our abilities to do all that it seems this new endeavor requires. But these "not enoughs" should never keep us from constructing that which the Lord instructs us to create. If His call is clear, He will make a way.

The Power of Reflection

You see, God never promised us that we would understand everything He calls us to construct. We may, in fact, be contributing to only part of something that we will never see completed. Our portion may simply be part of a larger whole that has a purpose He has not revealed to anyone yet. But once God makes His instruction clear, we must get busy obeying.

What's the largest "building project" God has called on you to construct so far? Where are you in the process of its construction?

....

....

....

....

....

....

....

....

What has been the cost of your participation in building this new thing? What resources has He provided along the way? Which ones are you still waiting for Him to provide?

....

....

....

....

....

....

....

....

How have those around you responded to what you're building? Who has provided encouragement and support?

....

....

....

....

....

....

....

How have you handled the people in your life who don't understand what you're about—or worse, those who stand in your way? How have you responded to the barriers they have placed in your path?

....

....

....

Noah and Mrs. Noah (as I like to call her) demonstrate a kind of tangible faith and practical obedience that we must never forget. In a culture intent on nothing except individual pleasure, sensual comforts, and selfish indifference to God (which might sound frighteningly like our culture today), Noah remained faithful, honest, and true. Whether or not he realized his integrity would be tested, he and his family nonetheless illustrate the way God delights in our obedience and often requires us to go against the grain of the society.

Noah didn't care what everyone else thought of his actions. He ignored their jokes, their mocking, their contempt and simply went about the business to which the Lord had very clearly called him. Instead of hesitating and worrying what others might think, Noah started doing the next thing that needed doing: cutting wood, sawing planks, making a boat larger than the world had ever seen.

What's the craziest or most spectacular request God ever has made of you? How did you respond? How did you verify that this instruction really was of God (Scripture, confirmation from more mature Christians, prayer, other circumstances)?

....

....

....

....

....

....

....

What's your usual response when God asks you to do something that will cause you to stand out from the crowd? How do you respond to those who don't understand?

....

....

....

....

....

....

....

....

What new thing is God calling you to accomplish
for Him? What new trail are you being asked to
blaze, or what new structure are you being asked
to build? How has God prepared you for this endeavor?

....

....

....

....

....

....

....

Noah wasted no time cutting timber, sawing planks, and preparing the pitch to hold his ark together. What preparations should you be making in order to construct your own Noah's ark–sized endeavor?

....

....

....

....

....

....

....

So often we hear God's voice directing us and then feel overwhelmed by what he's asking us to construct. . . . We come up with excuses and indicate why we can't do something instead of demonstrating Noah-style faith, a faith that floats.

—You Have It in You!, page 114

The Power of His Word

Noah's story is one of those familiar tales of God's doing something impossible through the obedience of one person. But as I point out in Chapter 6, in order to heed God's call on your life and live out your divine destiny, you usually need the support, understanding, and encouragement of your family and other loved ones. While we don't know Mrs. Noah's story, it's clear that she didn't stand in her husband's way and was willing, literally, to get on board this crazy thing that God had asked him to build.

While I believe we each have our own ark we're called to build, I'm also convinced that we are called to support the constructions of those around us. Mrs. Noah could've been just as incredulous, embarrassed, or contemptuous as everyone else around her husband. But she stood by him and trusted that God had indeed spoken to him, no matter how unbelievable the request sounded. She didn't say, "But Noah, no one has ever built a boat that big!" or "Honestly, honey, a *flood*? Really? When there's not a cloud in the sky?"

Her faith was just as strong as his was in supporting the ark's construction as well as rounding up pairs of animals and sailing away. She may not have known she had it in her to trust what God was up to, but she knew that whatever Noah was doing, sink or float, she was going to be with him.

Read Noah's story in Genesis 5–10. Which surprises you more: God's anger and displeasure with people or Noah's no-questions-asked willingness to build the ark? Which is easier for you to handle in your own life, God's judgment or His mercy?

....

....

....

....

....

....

....

Where is God calling you to take a stand in your life, even if others ridicule you? Who are the people in your life He is asking you to support and trust just as Mrs. Noah stood by Noah?

....

....

....

....

....

....

....

....

And God said: "This is the sign of the covenant which I make between Me and you, and every living creature that is with you, for perpetual generations: I set My rainbow in the cloud, and it shall be for the sign of the covenant between Me and the earth."

(Gen. 9:12–13 NKJV)

The Power to Change

Many people will never understand our faith in God and why we do what we do for Him. They may dismiss us as "religious fanatics" or "Jesus freaks" or call us names far worse. They may say we're crazy or silly or naive or stupid for obeying the call of God on our lives. They may rely only on what they can see, hear, touch, taste, and feel and disbelieve anything revealed by God's Spirit. Sometimes their ridicule will hurt more than others, especially if it comes from family or people we thought were our friends.

Regardless of what others think of us, though, we must never allow their opinions to influence our thoughts and actions more than God and His Word. The people in Noah's day had given up on God, so the Bible tells us (see Gen. 6). All except Noah and his family. Just like Adam, Noah became a new forefather for all of us who have followed after him. God used Noah's faithful obedience to influence the course of history as part of His divine plan.

Which area of your life have you allowed to be more influenced by popular culture and other people than by God's standards? In what areas of your life do you need to make changes today in order to be used by God tomorrow? Is there something you're doing as a regular habit? What you watch on TV or in movie theaters? The music you listen to? The people you hang around?

....

....

....

....

....

....

Make a list of the habits, thoughts, and behaviors in your life that you know are not pleasing God. Spend some time in prayer asking Him for His mercy and forgiveness. What do you need to do now in order to move beyond these old barriers and move forward with constructing a new life?

....

....

....

....

....

....

....

....

The Power of Prayer

Lord, you know where I've fallen short of all You ask me to do. Please forgive me for these sins and allow me to start fresh, just as You gave the world a fresh start after the flood. Give me the strength, courage, and integrity of Noah and his wife so I can build something that will rise above the selfish culture around me, something that will glorify You and point others to Your loving kindness. Please show me whom to trust in this endeavor and provide me with your wisdom and discernment as I take steps to obey Your call. Remind me, God, that even when the floodwaters are rising around me, there's always a rainbow after the storm. Amen.

> Sometimes even after we've completed the assignment God has given us, we must remain patient. We still have to work hard and remain obedient as we wait for our next assignment. We can't just rest on our big accomplishment as the pinnacle of our lives. Sometimes we have to ride out the storm, perhaps even realizing that what God has called us to build is the means of our survival.
>
> —*You Have It in You!*, page 121

CHAPTER SEVEN

More Than a Maid
Serving with the Humility
of Naaman's Maid

Before you begin: Please familiarize yourself with
Chapter 7 of *You Have It in You!*, pages 125–145.

T HERE'S AN OLD song that reminds us, "Little things mean
a lot." And certainly in a relationship with your spouse
or kids or someone you love, the small details really do add
up. Whether it's taking out the trash without being asked,
surprising someone with a little note tucked in with his or
her lunch, or giving an unexpected bouquet of flowers, it's
amazing the effect that something seemingly small can have
on another person.

But these "big little things" don't have to be exclusive to

our immediate circle of loved ones. Sometimes they don't even come from someone we know, let alone someone we love. And sometimes a complete stranger's kindness has more power to stun us with God's love than a gift from someone who knows us. It may be a supportive smile from someone in the group when you're speaking or teaching, a cup of coffee for a coworker who's overwhelmed, or a handful of dollar bills for a person in need at the intersection. In fact, I'm convinced that we rarely grasp the enormous impact one small, kind gesture can have in terms of changing someone else's day or even life.

The Power of Reflection

Maybe it's because I'm sensitive, or because God continues to allow His compassion to flow through me, but I'm usually aware of and especially grateful for the people who serve my ministry and me each day. From the barista at the coffee shop who never fails to smile to the members of our congregation who surprise me with love and support me with their prayers, I couldn't do all that God calls me to do without all of the ingredients they contribute to any given day. It's a good reminder that everything I offer can have the same kind of effect on those around me.

How often do you sense God using you to impact those around you—including strangers—on a daily basis? When was the last time you immediately responded to God's prompting and did or said something to help someone?

....

....

....

....

....

....

Think back over your day today or the day before. How would the people you encountered—your family, your coworkers, your friends, your child's teacher, the waitress at the café, the members of your prayer group, everyone—describe their interactions with you?

....

....

....

....

....

....

....

....

When was the last time someone's unexpected gift of kindness changed your mood or the kind of day you were having? What did the person do that made his or her act memorable? How did you respond?

....

....

....

....

....

....

....

If you're honest, are there certain people (perhaps your boss or pastor, a political leader or person in authority) you treat better than others? Similarly, are there people you regularly encounter whom you rarely think about as people? The airline attendant, the sales rep, the valet in the parking lot, the babysitter, the checkout clerk at the market all need to see God's love through you as much as anyone else.

....

....

....

....

....

....

....

....

If anyone could be justified for not displaying the patience, kindness, and compassion of the Lord, it seems likely that a prisoner of war forced to be a servant would fit the bill.

Yet as we see in the story of Naaman's little maid, she refused to let her circumstances rob her of her dignity, integrity, and generosity of spirit. Despite the fact that she was now serving her foreign captors in Aram (Syria), she clearly came to care about the well-being of the family she served, including that of her master, Naaman, who suffered from leprosy.

Thanks to her faith in God and her confidence in His goodness, this young woman risked speaking up and offering a most unconventional solution. At the end of his rope with such a deadly disease, Naaman felt he had nothing to lose. He had already exhausted all other treatments and remedies, so why not return to the land of Israel and see the holy man recommended by his maid? What if it was his only hope?

Does someone in your life need your help, even if you feel reluctant to offer it? Who? What kind of aid can you offer?

....

....

....

....

....

What do you think prevents you from offering yourself in service to others? Wounds from your past? A lack of self-confidence? Fear of their response? Something else?

....

....

....

....

....

....

Do you know the name of the person who usually serves you at your favorite restaurant? Do you know anything about his or her family, needs, dreams, or goals? What's required for you to view this person as a fellow child of God rather than as your waiter or waitress?

....

....

....

....

....

....

....

....

When was the last time you sensed God calling
you to serve someone you considered "above" you?
Maybe it was your boss or pastor, someone famous
or wealthy. How did this person respond to what
you offered? How did you feel in turn?

....

....

....

....

....

....

> *We may feel insignificant, underappreciated, and overlooked. But everything we do matters, and sometimes God uses a small hinge to open an enormous door.*
>
> —*You Have It in You!*, page 127

The Power of His Word

So often when we find ourselves in the midst of a trial or crisis, the last thing we're thinking about is helping those around us, especially if they contributed to our current state of distress. But Naaman's maid had a perspective that was bigger than her immediate circumstances. Instead of feeling sorry for herself and moping about her captivity, she apparently cultivated relationships with her master's family and embraced the situation as an opportunity to be a true servant—not just to her foreign captors, but to her loving Father.

Naaman, on the other hand, also has something to teach us. As the leader of his king's successful army, he was used to the perks and privileges that came with being a VIP. But he discovered that a disease such as leprosy offers no special exclusions based on status or wealth. He may have been able to afford better treatment than others, but in the end, his body still suffered in the excruciating grasp of this deadly affliction. Then, when his maid offered a lifeline—Elisha, a prophet of God back in Israel—Naaman knew he had no other choice if he wanted to live and overcome his painful condition.

Elisha's method of treatment, at least from the famous general's point of view, went against common sense, disrespected his elite status, and repulsed his sense of propriety. Still, as Naaman's other servants reminded him, he truly had everything to gain. So he swallowed his pride and lost much more than the disease of leprosy as he bathed in the River Jordan. He lost his sense of entitlement.

In 2 Kings 5:1–19, you'll find the story of Naaman and his wife's young maid who ended up saving her master's life. Read through the story and consider this: Is it easier for you to relate to the humility of Naaman's maid or the entitlement of her important master? Why?

....

....

....

....

....

....

....

....

....

What is God asking you to do for Him that requires you to humble yourself? Whom is He asking
you to serve with an act of kindness today?

....

....

....

....

....

....

....

....

Now Naaman, commander of the army of the king of Syria, was a great and honorable man in the eyes of his master, because by him the Lord had given victory to Syria. He was also a mighty man of valor, but a leper. And the Syrians had gone out on raids, and had brought back captive a young girl from the land of Israel. She waited on Naaman's wife. Then she said to her mistress, "If only my master were with the prophet who is in Samaria! For he would heal him of his leprosy."

(2 Kings 5:1–3 NKJV)

The Power to Change

So much of our world revolves around wealth, status, and privilege. Popular culture trains us to judge others by their designer clothes, their expensive cars, and their flashy jewelry. But God's Word reminds us that we are all human, sons and daughters of our Creator, and no one is better than anyone else. In the New Testament, James explicitly told us not to show any favoritism between the rich and poor (Jam. 2:1). And we're repeatedly told, even by Jesus Himself, to love our neighbor as ourselves (Matt. 22:39). If we are to discover all that God has placed inside of us, then we must also realize that humility is often our tool for this discovery.

In what areas of your life do you think your prideful ego prevents you from discovering all that the Lord wants to give you: at work? Home? Church? In certain relationships? Ask God to reveal where your pride is getting in the way of what He wants to do.

....

....

....

....

....

....

....

....

....

Based on the areas you've just identified, what steps do you need to take today in order to humble yourself and allow God to work through you? Do you need to ask for forgiveness or apologize to someone? Perform an act of service or offer a gift of kindness? Something else?

....

....

....

....

....

....

....

....

The Power of Prayer

Lord, I know it's easy for me to focus more on my own problems and needs than those of the people around me. Please help me to be a person of humility, a servant to You through acts of service for everyone around me. Keep me focused on what unites us as people rather than the differences we allow to drive us apart. Help me to see others as You see them and to serve them with the love, compassion, and mercy that come only from You. Amen.

When our pride is washed from us, we are often healed from a number of our infirmities. Our pride can make our hearts hard and our souls sour. Sometimes, like Naaman, we must go to a place that's familiar and ordinary, a place we might even think is beneath us. God will do whatever it takes to humble us so that we turn our hearts to him instead of our wealth, position, or fame.

—*You Have It in You!*, page 139

CHAPTER EIGHT

COAT OF CONFIDENCE
Trusting with the Confidence of Joseph

Before you begin: Please familiarize yourself with
Chapter 8 of *You Have It in You!*, pages 147–165.

H AVE YOU EVER known anyone who was color-blind?
Apparently, individuals suffering from this condition cannot see the same color spectrum, especially red and
green, that the rest of us enjoy. Can you imagine not being
able to distinguish the colors in a beautiful rose garden or a
Christmas parade? Not being able to see the full beauty of a
rainbow after a spring shower? While not life-threatening,
color-blindness certainly robs its sufferers of the rich palette
with which God painted the world.

We may not be color-blind, but sometimes we lose sight of the vivid hues around us. Trial after trial occurs, and we go from one painful circumstance to another without any break in between. Before we can fully recover from one blow, we're hit again by betrayal, loss, or injustice. God begins to seem distant and aloof, and we don't understand why we continue to suffer. Our colorful lives start to look like an old black-and-white movie.

The Power of Reflection

In Chapter 8, I describe the amazingly beautiful quilt that a dear lady in my church made and gave to me. With its assorted fabrics, remnants, and textiles, the quilt displays the sharp contrast of soft pastels against bold blocks of color as well as the sensation of worn cotton against pieces of wool and silk. I love this quilt for many reasons, but I'm especially grateful for the way it reminds me of the way our lives resemble a crazy quilt of equally diverse colors and fabrics.

We often want each piece of our lives to be a perfect square, uniform and consistent with all the other pieces, flawless and harmonious in the way each connects to another. If things are going well—we enjoy our jobs, our families are healthy, the bills are paid—we want them to stay that way.

The reality, however, is that each day offers a new experience, a new part of our quilt that might be similar to what came before it or might take our breath away with its startling difference. Instead of trying to control the pieces and the making of our lives' quilts, I'm convinced the key is trusting our Creator with the materials as He transforms us into His masterpieces, knowing that even scraps of our most painful days can be redeemed through God's artistry.

Maybe your life doesn't feel like a quilt as much as another image or metaphor. As you look back on all the ups and downs—and on God's faithfulness holding everything together—how would you describe your life? What would you compare it to?

....

....

....

....

....

....

Name one of the major qualities you've discovered about yourself in the past year. Are you especially resilient? Compassionate? Are you a gifted teacher or wordsmith?

....

....

....

....

....

....

....

What strength or gift have you discovered in yourself that you continue to exercise in order to pursue God's call on your life?

....

....

....

....

....

....

....

....

Name one of the weaknesses or deficits you've discovered in yourself in the past year. What do you feel you're lacking that's needed to move forward into your divine destiny?

....

....

....

....

....

....

....

....

In what ways are you still the person you were as a child? What essential qualities remain in you as an adult: Curiosity? Leadership? Humility? Something else? How have you changed the most from childhood to the person you are now?

....

....

....

....

....

....

....

....

No one knew what it was like to ride life's roller coaster better than Jacob's youngest son, Joseph. On the one hand, he seems like one of the most talented, resourceful leaders in the Bible—in the right place at the right time to save Egypt from the devastations of famine. If you consider Joseph's life from another angle, however, it seems like a real-life soap opera, with one tragic cliff-hanger after another.

Betrayed by his jealous brothers, sold into captivity, falsely accused by a scheming seductress, and imprisoned as an innocent man—through it all, Joseph never lost sight of what God had placed in him. Even in the most desperate of situations, he knew that that with which others intended to harm him would be used by God to bless him.

What gift, talent, or ability is in you that seems to intimidate others the way Joseph's dreams intimidated his brothers?

....

....

....

....

....

....

....

....

....

How do you usually respond when those around you refuse to respect the gifts God has given you?

....

....

....

....

....

....

....

Describe a time in your life when you went from a high to a low very quickly, from a wonderful time of blessing to a time of adversity. In what ways did this contrast make overcoming the challenge harder? Easier?

....

....

....

....

....

....

....

....

When has God provided for your safety and protection during a trial or season of difficulty? How
did this change your perspective?

....

....

....

....

....

....

....

....

....

As we see in Joseph's story, when the mark of God is on your life, there can be definite dreams, or visions, associated with it. But be careful with whom you share them, because along with every God-given concept comes an "assassin" who wants to smother it before you can ever bring it to life.

—You Have It in You!, page 151

The Power of His Word

Joseph's story is one that never ceases to give us hope and courage in the face of hard times. One of the ways our spiritual enemy tries to weaken us is by isolating us in the midst of our trials. If the devil can make us feel sorry for ourselves, lonely and afraid, then we're more likely to become self-centered and to stop being God-centered. But even as we see Joseph enduring one twist and turn after another, he never gave up on God. He knew God had gifted him with a special destiny, had placed within him unique and powerful qualities.

Joseph's story involves a dream literally come true! And notice the way he maintained his integrity and trust every step of the way. When sold into slavery, he could have hardened his heart and decided to steal from his new master, Potiphar, or even take advantage of the situation with Potiphar's wife. But Joseph refused to be someone he was not. Similarly, in jail he could've become old and bitter before his time, giving up hope that God would free him, let alone elevate him to a position of prominence. But a small seed of kindness Joseph planted—interpreting his fellow prisoner's dream—ended up yielding a huge harvest.

Read Genesis Chapters 37, 39–45, and 50 in your favorite version of the Bible. Which part of Joseph's story seems the most painful? Which betrayals or injustices in his life remind you of ones from your own life?

....

....

....

....

....

....

....

How have you managed to stay true to who you know God wants you to be in the face of adversity? How has God blessed you along the way in the midst of hard times?

....

....

....

....

....

....

Joseph said to them, "Do not be afraid, for am I in the place of God? But as for you, you meant evil against me; but God meant it for good, in order to bring it about as it is this day, to save many people alive. Now therefore, do not be afraid; I will provide for you and your little ones." And he comforted them and spoke kindly to them.

(Gen. 50:19–21 NKJV)

The Power to Change

Perhaps the most striking feature of Joseph's story is that he refused to exact revenge on his brothers when finally given the opportunity. Arguably, none of the terrible events and injustices in his life would have occurred if his jealous brothers hadn't thrown him in a pit and then sold him to strangers. Surely, Joseph must have wondered what his life would have been like if he had remained in his homeland, in his father's house.

Still, Joseph was wise enough to realize he would never have ended up in Egypt in such a powerful position if not for the strange chain of events that led him to Pharaoh's palace. That others intended to destroy Joseph only made him stronger through the power of God's goodness and grace. As painful as his journey may have been, Joseph knew that God never abandoned him. He knew that despite how dark the world may have looked from his jail cell, life was still as colorful as the bright coat his father had once given him.

What keeps you motivated when everything around you seems to fall apart? What gets you through a day filled with painful surprises? What do you need to do today to strengthen your faith for tomorrow?

....

....

....

....

....

....

....

....

Make a list of the trials, obstacles, challenges, and losses that God has brought you through in your life. How has God used these painful seasons to reveal what's truly inside you? What have you discovered about yourself through them? As you move forward and face new challenges, remember all you have survived with God's help so far in life. Never forget that you're a survivor!

....

....

....

....

....

....

....

....

The Power of Prayer

Sometimes I feel as though I've reached my limit, that I can't bear any more arguments at home, conflicts at work, drama with friends, and even problems at church. Through it all, please help me to stay focused on You and Your plan for my life. Remind me that no matter how painful the storm, I will survive. I know You work all things together for good for those who love you. I love You so much, Lord, and even though it doesn't make sense, I trust that You are leading me to a special place of purpose, just as You did with Joseph. No matter how black and white and gray the world around me seems, never let me lose my ability to see my true colors. Amen.

The trial or painful circumstance that ensnares you right now may feel like a prison sentence. But we must never lose hope that he is orchestrating even the bad things into catalysts for his kingdom. Even when our world becomes black and white, as long as we have our coat of confidence, we will experience God's favor in living color.

—*You Have It in You!*, page 165

CHAPTER NINE

WHAT A DIFFERENCE A DAY MAKES

Waiting with the Patience of David

Before you begin: Please familiarize yourself with Chapter 9 of *You Have It in You!*, pages 167–188.

M OST PEOPLE DON'T think of the "good old days" as right now. Even if we endured hard times in the past, so often it's tempting to look over our shoulders and assume the best times are behind us. We reminisce about when we were younger, when we started our career, when we first got married, when the kids were little, or when we lived in that little shoebox home that wasn't much to look at. If we're honest, we know at the time so many of the events that we now look back on fondly were really painful.

Just as it's tempting to look at the past through rose-colored glasses, it's also easy to look at the future with fear. We start worrying about what could or might happen, what if this person went away or this person moved back into our lives, and we get scared. We worry about how we'll cope and whether we'll have enough time, money, strength, health, and support to get through the potential challenges we see looming on the horizon.

The Power of Reflection

When the past looks rosy and the future looks scary, we often miss out on what God has for us today. We become discouraged and stagnant, locking ourselves into lives scripted only by the things we can see or imagine, instead of trusting that all things—even the impossible—can happen with God. You think you know what's going to happen in your life today—work, home, school, church, the same old same old—but everything can change just like that.

Even though our lives may feel routine, we must remember that God is always working out His purposes. In a matter of moments, He can reveal the truth of who we are and uncover the power He's placed within us. We must never lose sight of where we're going, no matter how many detours we make along the way.

When you were growing up, did you ever imagine that you would be where you are now? How much of your life resembles any of what you expected even ten years ago?

....

....

....

....

....

....

....

....

....

....

....

When you consider the past and smile about your glory days, what events come to mind? Looking back, when do you think you were most content?

....

....

....

....

....

....

....

Based on where you are right now in your life, where will you be this time next year? Three years from now? Five years from now? Do you honestly think this is where God is leading you? Why or why not?

....

....

....

....

....

....

....

....

....

With these possibilities for your future in mind,
where do you really want to be one year from now?
Five? Where do you think God wants to lead you?

....

....

....

....

....

....

....

....

....

....

Whenever I get impatient, the story of David the shepherd boy whom God selected to be His king remains one of my favorites. Not only did David live a remarkably colorful, turbulent life, he also knew a thing or two about waiting on God's timing. Anointed by the prophet Samuel when he was still a teenager, David knew he was special and chosen by God to lead the nation of Israel. He also realized very quickly that just because he was anointed didn't mean he would become king overnight.

In fact, David had to wait a long time before the throne was his. And he had to endure a lot of hardship, disappointment, and persecution (from the old king whom David was replacing) along the way. But somehow David never gave up hope or demanded that the royal coronation be sped up. He waited on God's timing. And I'm convinced that whenever he grew impatient or complacent, David simply remembered what a difference a day makes.

How aware are you of God's using you in your present location and life circumstances? Do you feel as if you're where God wants you or that He's leading you somewhere else?

....

....

....

....

....

....

How often have you thought, If God is really leading me to my divine destiny, then life shouldn't be
so hard? How do you usually respond?

....

....

....

....

....

....

....

....

What's the hardest part of waiting on God? Are you more likely to expect to be disappointed by what He's about to reveal or thrilled by it?

....

....

....

....

....

....

....

....

As the youngest, David was overlooked by his father and brothers until Samuel inquired about him. How important is it to you that the people around you recognize your anointing?

....

....

....

....

....

....

....

....

> *Our lives may appear to be mundane and
> uneventful on the surface, but God is still working
> out his purposes for the good of those who love him.
> And in the twinkling of an eye, he can reveal
> the truth of who we are and uncover the power
> he's placed within us. And if he reveals our true
> identities to us early in life, we must never forget that
> anointing, even if it seems it couldn't be further from
> where we find ourselves now.*
>
> —*You Have It in You!*, page 170

The Power of His Word

Another reason David's story resonates so powerfully stems from the statement God made to Samuel as the prophet assessed David's brother: "Do not look at his appearance or at his physical stature, because I have refused him. For the Lord does not see as man sees; for man looks at the outward appearance, but the Lord looks at the heart" (1 Sam. 16:7 NKJV). While it's clear that the rest of his family considered David too young, too inexperienced, too naive, and untested, God made clear that His standards are different from those we use.

Too often we assume that the people God has chosen and blessed meet the world's standards of success. While this can be true, the two sets of criteria don't always intersect. God looks at what's inside us and knows, as our Creator, what He has placed there. No matter how we look to the people around us, God sees so much more. He knows how much strength we have, how much courage, patience, resilience, and faith. He knows the full extent of what we're made of long before we do.

David's family didn't consider him worthy even to mention to Samuel during his search for the next king. When has someone tried to discount your contribution or dismiss your ability to serve? How did you respond? How did you experience God's presence in the situation?

....

....

....

....

....

....

....

On the other hand, Samuel was listening to God and not to David's family, so he had no trouble recognizing and anointing the shepherd boy as king. Whom has God spoken to on your behalf recently? How has his or her support and encouragement enabled you to move forward in your divine destiny?

....

....

....

....

....

....

....

....

Read the story of David's anointing in 1 Samuel 16:1–13. You might also want to read more about David's life throughout various other seasons of his life as well as some of the beautiful psalms he composed. As you may know, King David lived a rich, robust life with as many ups and downs as anyone has ever experienced. Through it all, however, he never lost sight of his love for the Lord and his awareness that God had chosen him to lead his people.

....

....

....

....

....

....

....

....

And Samuel said to Jesse, "Are all the young men here?" Then he said, "There remains yet the youngest, and there he is, keeping the sheep."

And Samuel said to Jesse, "Send and bring him. For we will not sit down till he comes here."

So he sent and brought him in. Now he was ruddy, with bright eyes, and good-looking. And the Lord said, "Arise, anoint him; for this is the one!"

Then Samuel took the horn of oil and anointed him in the midst of his brothers; and the Spirit of the Lord came upon David from that day forward.

(1 Sam. 16:11–13 NKJV)

The Power to Change

Too often we don't walk through the doors God opens for us because we're afraid we're not qualified. We think we need a business degree to start a new company or a seminary education to preach God's Word. If we don't have the right clothes or live in the right part of town, we assume others won't recognize God's favor upon us. But David reminds us that no matter what we have or don't have on the outside of our lives, what we have on the inside matters most. This is why our best times need not be in the past. This is why we shouldn't be afraid of the future. God is in control of both and has given us everything we need to serve Him and be the best we can be.

When was the last time someone asked you to step up and instead of taking the risk, you made excuses? What do you assume you lack to serve God?

....

....

....

....

....

....

....

....

....

What's the source of your confidence regarding the
direction your life is taking? What risk do you need
to take today in order to stop making excuses and
instead boldly accept God's anointing on your life?

....

....

....

....

....

....

....

....

The Power of Prayer

Lord, I know You've chosen me for something special, for a unique and amazing role in Your kingdom's work. And I realize that those around me, even my family and friends, may not understand or see in me what You see. Help me to let go of the past and never to fear the future. Thank You for this day that You've given me, right here, right now. Grant me the confidence, God, to walk worthy of Your calling and to wait patiently on Your timing. Amen.

It's time to let go of all the false expectations and unnecessary conditions you've placed on yourself. It's time to let go of all the baggage of past mistakes and missed opportunities. It's time to move beyond the pitfalls of the past and the perfectionism of the present. It's time to keep your divine appointment with your God-given destiny!

—*You Have It in You!*, page 182

CHAPTER TEN

HOPE FOR THE HUNGRY HEART

Growing with the Honesty of Elijah

Before you begin: Please familiarize yourself with Chapter 10 of *You Have It in You!*, pages 189–217.

D O YOU ENJOY a good mystery story? You know, the kind where someone commits a crime and then an investigator collects clues until the mystery is solved? It may be a police officer or a private detective, a Sherlock Holmes type or a Nancy Drew, but in these stories someone is always smart enough to figure things out. If only life were so simple! There's something very satisfying about knowing that all the little clues mean something and form a pattern that reveals the truth of the situation.

I'm convinced many people enjoy mystery stories because rarely in life are solutions so easily uncovered. Even as we grow in our trust of the Lord, many events in our lives make us scratch our heads and wonder what God's up to. Sometimes in hindsight, even years later, we realize that some of the valleys we endured were necessary to reach the mountaintops. For many of us, though, we may have certain experiences that we're never able to figure out in this lifetime.

The Power of Reflection

Even when we're suffering through hardship, loss, disease, or depression, we must never forget the goodness of the Lord. Even when we can't understand why He's taken home someone we love or allowed a catastrophic event to occur, we should accept the limitations of our understanding and acknowledge God's sovereignty and loving kindness. Just because we don't understand what's going on doesn't mean that God doesn't have a plan. It simply means that we can't see the divine pattern He's currently weaving in the tapestry of our lives.

What pain in your life makes you wonder what God is doing? What is making you shrug your shoulders and struggle to understand what's going on?

....

....

....

....

....

....

When you first committed your life to God, did you expect to suffer as many hardships as you've experienced? Or did you assume that life might be easier with God on your side?

....

....

....

....

....

....

....

....

How has your past suffering shaped your present
strengths? What have you overcome with God's
help that continues to empower your resolve to
trust Him and move forward?

....

....

....

....

....

....

....

....

What's the biggest life change or loss you've experienced that continues to haunt your heart at times? What have you endured that you suspect you may never understand in this lifetime? How do you handle the pain of such a situation?

....

....

....

....

....

....

....

In Chapter 10, I explain some of the painful losses I endured early in my life, including the death of my father when I was eleven years old. These kinds of wounds often shape us for the rest of our lives. And while we may not have any control over the circumstances themselves, we always have a choice about our response. Our enemy, the devil, wants us to view ourselves as powerless victims who have no choice but to give up. He wants to rob us of our hope.

God, however, will sustain us if we let Him. His Word reminds us that we are not victims but victors! The only difference between the two is usually our perception. If we feel paralyzed by our pasts, then we're going to lose sight of where we are today and where we're going tomorrow. If we view ourselves as powerless, then we've basically allowed our yesterdays to dictate our tomorrows. But it doesn't have to be this way. No matter what kind of suffering we experience, there is always hope. God never abandons us and we are never far from His love.

> What defining events from your childhood continue to impact your life today? What losses have you seen God redeem or transform into blessings? Which ones are you still waiting to see transformed?

....

....

....

....

....

....

....

....

....

What's the most precious thing you've ever lost
and then had restored: Your health? Your marriage?
Your career? Your reputation? How would you describe the process now, as you look back from this
side of it?

....

....

....

....

....

....

....

....

....

What personal dream would you like to see God revive and bring to life? How would your life be different if He resurrected your dream today?

....

....

....

....

....

....

When has God granted you His peace about certain events that you still don't understand? How have you experienced His presence even during your doubts and losses?

....

....

....

....

....

....

....

....

> *Everything you endure, encounter, and conquer—*
> *even those things you feel are conquering you right*
> *now—is for a reason. God wastes nothing in our*
> *lives and is always redeeming even the most painful*
> *of situations.*
>
> —*You Have It in You!*, page 193

The Power of His Word

The story of Elijah would not make a very good mystery story. He faced lots of hard situations without many clues about what God was working on. And yet the prophet, for all his moaning and groaning, kept going and kept experiencing the power and provision of the Lord. Whether it was daily food from the ravens, the amazing supply of flour in the widow's cupboard, or the resurrection of her son after a deadly illness, Elijah constantly relied on God.

Like most of us, Elijah wasn't always happy about it. As God's prophet, a holy man often recognized and revered in his culture, Elijah may have expected a very different set of circumstances from the roller coaster he experienced. Nonetheless, he discovered a deeper faith, a deeper confidence, a deeper hope in his relationship with God than he could have experienced otherwise. As excruciating as certain seasons of our lives may be, we must realize that suffering is part of what equips us for our divine destiny. I think of these periods as "training sessions" that make us tougher and take us to new levels of faith and spiritual maturity.

Check out the story of Elijah in 1 Kings 17. From your perspective, what's the hardest thing Elijah endured? Which of his trials hits closest to home or parallels one you've been through?

....

....

....

....

....

....

How has God used past training sessions to equip
you for what you're facing right now? In what area
of your life have you grown the most?

....

....

....

....

....

....

....

....

So she said, "As the Lord your God lives, I do not have bread, only a handful of flour in a bin, and a little oil in a jar; and see, I am gathering a couple of sticks that I may go in and prepare it for myself and my son, that we may eat it, and die."

And Elijah said to her, "Do not fear; go and do as you have said, but make me a small cake from it first, and bring it to me; and afterward make some for yourself and your son.

"For thus says the Lord God of Israel: 'The bin of flour shall not be used up, nor shall the jar of oil run dry, until the day the Lord sends rain on the earth.'"

So she went away and did according to the word of Elijah; and she and he and her household ate for many days.

The bin of flour was not used up, nor did the jar of oil run dry, according to the word of the Lord which He spoke by Elijah.

(1 Kings 17:12–16 NKJV)

The Power to Change

If you find yourself in the midst of a training session, try to step outside the circumstances and gain a larger perspective. Remember that God is still in control, no matter how hard things seem, and that He has not abandoned you. Accept that He is preparing you for something greater, something you may not even be able to imagine right now. As painful as each punch feels, hold on to God and trust Him to bring you through this storm stronger than ever. Give Him thanks and praise for all He's doing and how well equipped you'll be to face what's ahead.

If you could ask God to reveal His purposes behind one particular situation in your life, which one would you choose? Why? How would your life be different if you understood His divine purpose?

....

....

....

....

....

....

....

....

Sometimes when we're in a training session, we overlook helping and serving others. We may feel like the widow who didn't have enough for herself and her son, let alone this strange man telling her to feed him first. But often God wants to teach us how to act on faith. Is there someone you should be serving today regardless of what you're experiencing right now? Where is God calling you to step out in faith as His ambassador?

....

....

....

....

....

....

....

The Power of Prayer

Lord, so often I find it easy to trust in You and follow Your voice. But then when it appears I hit a dead end, I begin to second-guess and wonder if I heard You correctly. Sometimes events make no sense and seem more mysterious and pointless than ever. In these moments, give me the strength to step forward in confidence, knowing that You are perfect in Your ways and sovereign in Your decisions. Help me to see Your provision and to become more resourceful and resilient through these trials. Allow me to rely on You and You alone, no matter what storms may rage around me. You tell me that I have what it takes to be more than a conqueror through Your power. I claim victory right now even as I step out in faith and discover more of what You have planted inside me. Amen.

When God breathes new life into your heart, you discover the grace to handle things you could not handle before. And once you've adjusted your perspective, you no longer see your situation as a place of trouble but as a place of training. Once your perspective changes, you know you're not going to be taken out of the fight, only toughened up for the next one.

—*You Have It in You!*, page 211

THE
ULTIMATE TREASURE

Discovering the Joy of God's Power

Before you begin: Please familiarize yourself with the
Conclusion of *You Have It in You!*, pages 219–225.

SOMETIMES THE PROCESS of discovering what God has
placed inside us is like participating in a scavenger hunt.
Maybe you remember going on scavenger hunts as a kid
or with friends as a young adult. You look for an item, and
when you find it, that item includes a clue that leads you
to the next one, and so on. Once we begin the process of
recognizing all that God has placed in us, we usually end up
discovering another gift, another strength, another part of
ourselves that we didn't know was there. We may think we

know all there is to know about ourselves, but God is just getting started!

As we've seen with our examples, from Ruth to Elijah, He gives each one of us more than we realize. He equips us for the challenges we're facing and blesses us with opportunities to excel. We may have only a vague glimpse of who we really are, but God knows and is committed to giving us a clear picture of ourselves as His sons and daughters. Scripture tells us, "He who began a good work in you will carry it on to completion until the day of Christ Jesus" (Phil. 1:6 NIV). God doesn't start something and leave it undone. He wants us to know our true worth and to shine like bright beacons in the darkness around us.

The Power of Reflection

Which of the following qualities are part of the treasure God has placed inside you? Check all that apply:

Compassion   ....

Hospitality   ....

Friendship   ....

Teaching ....

Leadership ....

Administration ....

Organization ....

Encouragement ....

Peacemaking ....

Wisdom ....

Entrepreneurial vision ....

Confidence ....

Patience ....

What other gifts are part of your treasure? How have you seen God use them recently?

....

....

....

....

....

....

....

As you think back over the people we've studied in *You Have It in You!*, which one intrigues you the most? Why?

....

....

....

....

....

....

....

....

Which one went through experiences most similar
to what you're now going through? What have you
learned about yourself from his or her experience?

....

....

....

....

....

....

....

....

The Power of His Word

In the Conclusion, I share with you one of my all-time favorite verses: He has "made known to us the mystery of His will, according to His good pleasure which He purposed in Himself" (Eph. 1:9 NKJV). This verse reassures me that knowing and understanding God's will for my life is a process, not a one-time event. It's a mystery, not a scientific formula or a casserole recipe. It occurs in moments of prayer and worship, of service and sacrifice, of tears and laughter.

Spend some time reflecting on this verse and its meaning in your life right now. You may want to commit it to memory or write it out on a sticky note that you can post and see every day.

The Power to Change

How has your perception of yourself changed since you began reading *You Have It in You!* and completing this workbook? What has surprised you the most about yourself?

....

....

....

....

....

....

....

....

Based on what you're learning about all that's inside you, where is God leading you to use your gifts?

....

....

....

....

....

....

....

The Power of Prayer

Heavenly Father, thank You for the treasure You've poured inside me. Thank You for the many gifts I haven't even discovered yet. Just as the saints in Scripture discovered that they had more in them than they realized, help me to trust You for all I need. I give You thanks and praise for how wonderfully made I am. You have created me unlike anyone else throughout all time and history. You have chosen me for a special destiny that only I can accomplish. Give me the patience to persevere when obstacles block my path or the enemy tries to distract me. Allow me to remember how much You love me and to continue on this powerful path no matter what gets in my way. Keep surprising me with new facets of who I am. Amen.

Believe him for the impossible, the unimaginable, the unobtainable. If he has called you to accomplish something, you can rely on it happening. Even when it doesn't happen according to your timetable, wait on him and do not grow faint. You are closer to your divine destiny than ever before. Don't give up a few minutes before the miracle! Don't let go of your grasp on greatness!

—You Have It in You!, page 224